What Do You Do When You Know That YOU'RE HOOKED?

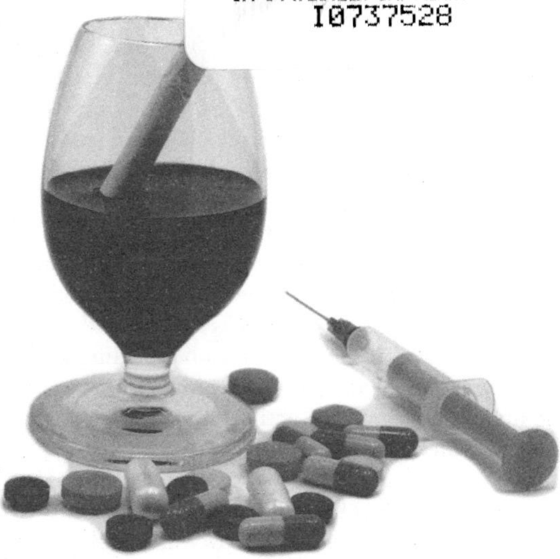

JAY E. ADAMS

the New Testament often calls it) is not some second work of grace subsequent to salvation; it is the result of the normal growth that ought to characterize every Christian's life. The filling issues forth in the building activities mentioned in verses 19–20, in contrast to the destructive outcome of the life of drunkenness. But—and this is of importance—the filling of the Spirit is not to be conceived of as a matter of how full or how empty one's cup may be (as if there could be a *half filling* or a *three-quarters filling*, etc.). Rather it is a matter of whether one is *dominated* and *controlled* by the Spirit or whether he is *under the influence* of alcohol. The filling is a spreading out of the influence of the Spirit of God into every area of the Christian's life. As He becomes dominant in each aspect of life, of course it is true that He dominates the Christian more and more. But unless His influence is paramount in *each* area of your life (that is, *fills* your life), you will find that it is not possible to replace the old way of life.

The old addiction to alcohol or to another addictive drug now dominates (or fills) your life. Its baneful influences reach into every nook and cranny of it, bringing the inevitable destruction that follows. Since addiction is thus a life-dominating sin (in passages like 1 Corinthians 6 God identifies people as "drunkards"—that is to say, their very lives can be characterized by the term), it reaches every area of life and its influence must be replaced by the Spirit's influence in the whole life.

A life-dominating sin acts upon and reacts to what occurs in every area of life. When Joe gets drunk (or stoned) he performs poorly at work. When he performs poorly at work he knows so (or is told so) and as a consequence begins to feel bad. This bad feeling is God's warning signal intended to bring him up short to examine and discontinue the activity that triggered it. But instead, since he feels bad, he hits the drug again to drown or alter the feeling. But getting drunk or getting high further impairs his ability to perform well at work. Thus the problem cycles. Moreover, his health suffers, his relationship with his wife suffers, and so on. As each incident in each of these additional areas arises, there are more reasons for bad feelings, which he wrongly tries in vain to handle with more of the drug. Thus other cycles interlace and crisscross previous ones until Joe, who is a whole person (i.e., whatever happens to him in one aspect of his life affects the rest of his life), at length finds that everything that he does contributes to the drug problem just as the drug problem contributes to failures in every area of his life. Thus the physical, family, church, that is inconsistent with drunkenness. A drug addict is still an addict until he has learned a new lifestyle that does not include drug abuse. At *every point* the new lifestyle must replace all the ways associated with the old one. When feeling low or disappointed or angry you found that previously this led to hitting the bottle. The new way, therefore, must include a new biblical way of handling these or other problems. If the old way of life centered around certain friendships and places where others engaged in like behavior (as the life of addiction usually does), then the new way must not merely require you to give up the old friendships and the old haunts, but it must go further and insist on developing new, strengthening ties of Christian fellowship. And it must center your activities on the home and the church (see 1 Cor. 15:33—"Do not be deceived: bad company ruins good morals"—and Heb. 10:24–25—"Let us consider how to stir up one another to love and to good works, not neglecting to assemble together as is the habit of some, but encouraging one another").

Now let us turn to a key biblical directive that describes this replacement dynamic in words plainly referring to your problem: "Do not get drunk with wine, for that is debauchery, but be filled with the Spirit" (Eph. 5:18). Notice that it contains not only the prohibition but also the alternative way of life. There is both a put off and a put on. One style of living is described as debauchery, the other as Spirit filled. The answer to all addiction, whether the drunkard's drug or other drugs used as mood changers for either depressing the spirit or for getting high, may be found in a life in which the Holy Spirit enables the believer to meet problems with wisdom and joy (see Eph. 5:19–20 and the parallel passage in Col. 3:16–17).

Let us contrast the two ways of life: the life of drunken debauchery and the life filled with the Spirit of wisdom and joy. What is meant by each? *Debauchery* is only one of a number of English words that have been used to represent a term that has no exact English equivalent. The Greek word, *asotia*, means literally "unsavable" and carries the connotation of a life ruined and destroyed by drunkenness. It is a life beyond reclamation. The picture is of a life of wild disorder that ends in thorough destruction. This, Paul warned, is the end result of drunkenness: it takes over and destroys everything. If drunkenness is not put to an end, soon everything else will be. On the other hand there is the life of joy and wise action motivated by the Holy Spirit. This *filling* of the Holy Spirit (as

WHAT DO YOU DO now that you are hooked . . . on alcohol or other drugs? By now you've tried nearly everything, but nothing helps. Sure, you can stay off the stuff for a few days—once you thought that you had it licked because you were dry for two weeks. But here you are again, caught by the habit—a man created by God to subdue the earth, instead hooked by a chemical! Is there no release?

Yes, there is. But the way out does not run in the directions that you have been travelling. There is one, and only one, way to put this problem permanently behind you: God's way.

First, let me show you what God says to a group of people who at one time like you were struggling with life-dominating problems. Notice that among those listed is the sin of addiction:

> Do not be deceived; neither the immoral, nor idolaters, nor adulterers, nor homosexuals, nor thieves, nor the greedy, nor *drunkards*, nor revilers, nor robbers will inherit the kingdom of God. And such *were* some of you. But you were washed, you were sanctified, you were justified in the name of the Lord Jesus Christ and by the Spirit of our God. (1 Cor. 6:9–11)

Did you get the full import of those words? Paul says, "Such *were* some of you." The verb is in the past tense. God made it possible for these Corinthian Christians to put away the problem of addiction once and for all; they were beyond it. And it was Jesus Christ, who by forgiving and cleansing and changing them through giving them His Spirit, had made it possible for them to do so. Notice, unlike other ways of dealing with the problem, Paul says that it can be cleared up once and for all. That means that he disagrees with those who say that every day for the rest of his life, the drunkard or the drug addict must tell himself, "I am an alcoholic" or "I am an addict," even after years of sobriety. Jesus offers no such halfway solution. He fully forgives and enables one to conquer these sins.

"How can Christ change me so that the change sticks?" you may ask. Good question. In fact, this question is a crucial one, isn't it? You don't want to be disappointed again. You don't want to raise your hopes once more only to find them dashed to pieces around your feet as they have been so often in the past. I don't blame you for that. Nor do I want this to happen to you. And it will not—if you are willing to follow God's way to the straight and sober pathway that leads to eternal life. Other ways failed you because they were not God's ways.

But whenever you truly depend upon the promises of God you can know that there will be no failure; God keeps His promises. That's why it is safe to hope once more.

"What makes the difference? Why did I go back to my old ways before? How will God's way keep me from doing so?" These questions probably are uppermost in your mind. So let us address our attention to them.

Basic to everything else, you must know God as a child knows His Father. If you have never become a member of the family of God, you are not eligible to enter into the promises of which I have been speaking. God has reserved His promises for His own children. You were born not into the family of God, but into the family of Satan, just like every other human being who was ever born on this earth by natural means. That means you must have a second birth if you are to become a member of the heavenly family. God by His Spirit brings conviction of sin and ability to believe in Jesus Christ as Savior. If He is making you conscious of the fact that your sins are an offense against God, that you are captive to them, and that you need forgiveness and power to overcome them, you need to trust Christ as Savior. How? By acknowledging your sins against God, recognizing that Christ came into the world to save His people from their sins, and putting your dependence upon Him. To be saved you must believe the good news that Christ bore the guilt and the punishment for all of your sins. In accordance with His own promise God raised Him from the dead, thus authenticating the fact that He accepted the substitutionary sacrifice of Christ. Unless you have had your sins forgiven and have become a member of God's family, what follows is not for you.

Now let us suppose that you have put your trust in the Lord Jesus Christ and that you know that your sins are forgiven—even the sin of addiction. The Holy Spirit of God dwells within you. You are God's temple (see 1 Cor. 6:19). That means that you must glorify God in your body; you must not defile or injure the temple of the Spirit. Addiction must go if you are to please God. You want to shake this old way, but you do not know how. You are pained that, although you have tried, you have failed as you did before you became a Christian. What do you do now?

Note that the Spirit of God lives in you. He has taken up residence for several purposes, one of which is to help you do things that you could not do without Him. One of these things is to understand the Scriptures and their meaning for your life (read 1 Cor. 2). He Himself is the Author of the Scriptures (2 Peter 1:20–21), and in that Book He has given the directions for overcoming your problem. As you read prayerfully, asking God for help to understand and with a willingness to please Him by doing whatever His Word says, the Spirit of God will make the way clear to you. Then, as you prayerfully step out in trusting obedience to do whatever the Scriptures require, the Spirit will give you the strength to accomplish what you wish. But, as you begin, be careful to set out with a desire to please God in this endeavor, not merely with the purpose of shaking off a troublesome habit. You must make pleasing Him your chief goal above all others. You must not use God to accomplish your purposes; you must accomplish His purposes so that you may be used by Him!

Now let's return to the matter of change that sticks. What makes the difference? Why do people go back to their old ways and fail to consolidate apparent gains? And how does biblical change avoid this failure? The answer lies in this: most systems teach addicts and drunkards to try to *quit* the undesirable practice. But that is plainly not enough. To quit taking heroin or boozing or smoking pot will not do the job. Sinful behavior must not be *stopped*; rather, God says that it must be *replaced*. Habits must not be *broken*; they must be *replaced* with new and righteous ones. When one only *stops* or *quits*, he is still an addict who (temporarily) is not engaged in the habit. Only when he *changes* by a reorganization and reorientation of his responses into a new pattern (or manner of life) can he be said to have undergone a change that will stick. There is, in the final analysis, no way to change permanently apart from positive change. Negative change (merely quitting, stopping, etc.) will not stick.

But where can one learn the new positive changes to make, and by what power can he replace old sinful ways with new holy ones? Only God, in His Word, can tell you what to do instead. It is only in the Bible that you can find the righteous style of life that is needed to replace the unrighteous one. Paul put it this way: "As you once yielded your [bodily] members to impurity and to greater and greater sin, so now yield your members to righteousness for further sanctification" (Rom. 6:19). In Colossians 3 and Ephesians 4 he says that you must "put off" (negative change) and "*put on*" (positive change). These words run throughout these two chapters. The behavior that is *put on* is that which must replace the behavior and attitudes that are *put off.*

Quitting is not changing, as we have seen. A drunk is still a drunk even when he is not drinking, and he will remain a drunk until he has learned a new way of life

Fourth, in accordance with the passage from 1 Corinthians 15 quoted above, you will find that it is necessary to avoid all future associations with any companions with whom you have previously indulged in the practice you seek to abandon. Cut off *all* connections *entirely*. You cannot resume any relationship with them until such a time as you have fully put on the new way of life. At that time, and at that time only, will you be strong enough to try to help them find God's road out of addiction. You may wish to argue about this matter, but there can be no argument. All such argument arises from serious self-deception. Remember the verse (and in particular, do not miss the import of the first four words): "Do not be deceived: bad company ruins good morals."

Fifth, using the list that you have composed, you must both structure every area of your life against all the old ways (how you do your work, how you speak to your wife, etc.) and also restructure it in ways that lead to new biblical alternatives to each practice. Here is where the Christian counsel of another is of essence. The form below may be of assistance to you and to him in developing ways and means of facilitating the new practices and impeding the old ones. Be specific and concrete when you fill it out.

Impediments and Facilitators

Impediments

To the former sinful ways

Add: ______________________________

____

____

____

____

To the new holy ways

Remove: ______________________________

____

____

____

____

____

____

____

____

____

____

____

____

____

____

Rehabituation list
(God says I must put on:)

____

____

____

____

____

____

____

____

____

____

____

____

Third, in effecting the change, work closely with someone who practices biblical counseling—a pastor, a chaplain, or some knowledgeable Christian worker who can help you through the difficult days of coming off of the drug or drugs to which you are now addicted. He also will be of help to you during the period in which you will need to restructure your entire life along biblical lines.

economic, social, occupational, and other, aspects of his life are all ultimately part of the lifestyle of a drunkard. It should not be difficult to see then how this filling out of one's life with alcohol or some other drug cannot be countered by an attempt to stop drinking or to kick the habit. That is why all such programs are doomed to failure. Instead, the only adequate way to be freed from a life-dominating sin is through life change in every area. And that is exactly what the Scriptures propose—that the entire life be restructured by the filling of the Spirit. Every area now dominated by the ruinous effects of sin must be changed so that instead it is daily benefited by the influences of the Spirit. Keeping this basic fact in mind, let us outline a simple program that will help any Christian to make the change that sticks.

First, repent of your sin to God, seeking His help to understand the Scriptures and to enable you to apply them accurately to your own life. Express genuine concern to do whatever God requires of you.

Second, probing into every area of your life, make a full list of concrete ways in which you are failing God and others. You should take time to compose this list since you will want to use it repeatedly throughout the days to come. Honesty and thoroughness are essential. The form that follows may help you to get started. Notice that it also provides for the biblical alternative to each sinful practice.

Change is a two-factored process

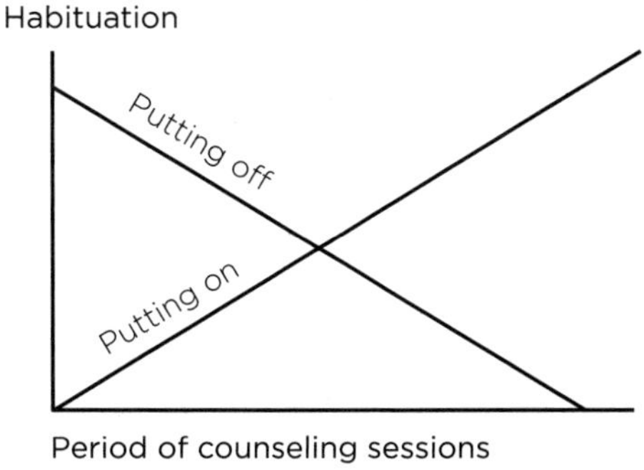

DEHABITUATION LIST
(God says I must put off:)

____

____

To the former sinful ways

Remove: ______________________________

____

____

____

____

To the new holy ways

Add: ______________________________

____

____

____

____

Now that you know what to do you must do it. Do not wait; start today. By the grace of God, you can unhook your addiction. It will not be easy, and there will be discouragements. But if you truly trust in Jesus Christ and do as he says, by His grace you will succeed. For further information concerning the put off / put on dynamic, read chapter 18 of the *Christian Counselor's Manual* by Jay E. Adams or contact P&R Publishing at P.O. Box 817, Phillipsburg, New Jersey 08865.

CHRISTIAN LIVING / COUNSELING
ISBN: 978-0-87552-047-6
EAN
9 780875 520476 50030

P&R PUBLISHING
www.prpbooks.com • 1-800-631-0094